Original title:
Wormhole Wanderlust

Copyright © 2025 Creative Arts Management OÜ
All rights reserved.

Author: Simon Fairchild
ISBN HARDBACK: 978-1-80567-833-5
ISBN PAPERBACK: 978-1-80567-954-7

Veins of the Universe

Through the cosmos I take flight,
Chasing stars that dance at night.
Planets waltz, I trip and swerve,
Is that a comet or a curve?

I meet a blob with googly eyes,
It offers snacks and cosmic fries.
I munch on nuggets made of space,
Then float in zero-gravity grace.

Quasars giggle, pulsars sing,
What a strange and wobbly thing!
Asteroids knock, it's an awkward game,
"Oh dear, did I break that fame?"

A black hole whispers, "Come on dear,
Just jump right in, don't show your fear."
I think of doughnuts, filled with cream,
But end up caught in a cosmic dream.

Immersed in Infinity

In a space where socks are lost,
And time forgot to count the cost.
We twirl through stars with silly glee,
Dodging meteors, oh look at me!

Galactic giggles fill the air,
With aliens who love to share.
They trade us snacks that float and bounce,
While gravity makes pancakes pounce.

A dance of planets, wobbly fun,
While comets race and light years run.
We laugh till we just can't catch breath,
In the whimsical, cosmic breadth.

So here we drift, no rules apply,
With silly hats that blow us high.
Infinity's a playful friend,
In laughter, let this journey blend.

Beyond the Light Years

Past the stars, where jokes are born,
And laughter sparkles like the dawn.
We surf on beams, not quite so straight,
While cosmic creatures play and skate.

A planet shaped like a giant shoe,
Where unicorns shine and dodos brew.
We sip on stardust, giggle and spin,
As wild adventures bubble within.

Time's a trickster, always late,
With calendars all out of state.
Each tick-tock brings a clever grin,
In orbits where our fun begins.

Through nebulae, we waltz around,
Without a care, lost and found.
In endless nights and countless days,
We dance through space in funny ways.

Drifting Through Dimensions

In a realm where dreams collide,
With rainbow slides and giddy rides.
We bounce through doors of time and space,
In socks that light up every place.

A twisty path of jelly beans,
Where nothing's ever as it seems.
With every flip and every turn,
The rules of physics take a burn.

Silly notes fly by our side,
As giggling time travelers glide.
Spaceships made of bubblegum,
Race each other: Zoom! Here they come!

Through rifts of color, we will soar,
With puns and winks galore, what's more!
In dimensions where the odd is king,
Let laughter be the song we sing.

Solstice Skylines

Beneath the sun in swirling skies,
We catch the rays of laughter's highs.
With flip-flops made of starlit threads,
We dance on rooftops, laugh instead.

Silly shadows chase us round,
In cosmic games, we've truly found,
That every breath we're bound to take,
Is filled with joy and silly breaks.

Floating past the twilight's glow,
We ride on beams, so fast they go.
With wishes whispered to the night,
We chase the giggles, oh what a sight!

So raise a toast to endless fun,
A universe where we have won.
In solstice glow, we spin and play,
In this bizarre, delightful way.

Beyond the Event Horizon

A lunchbox floats in space, oh dear,
It seems Sam's sandwich disappeared!
With jelly stars and bread so light,
He's lost his meal in cosmic flight.

The galaxy glows with neon rays,
While Sam does a dance in zero ways.
He twirls and spins through the cosmic zone,
While munching on snacks he thought he'd own.

The planets giggle, wobble, and sway,
As his lunch floats further away.
With no gravity holding it tight,
Sam's sandwich ventures out of sight.

Yet he won't fret, he'll find a new snack,
In this strange realm, there's no turning back.
He'll feast on moon dust, or comet ice cream,
In the universe's bizarre, silly dream.

Cosmic Highways

On the cosmic roads, with no stop signs,
Traffic's light, and that's just fine.
Aliens zoom in shiny cars,
While they snack on interstellar bars.

A traffic jam—wait, what's that smell?
It's just some space cheese that fell from a shell.
Drivers sing tunes of their favorite hits,
As they dodge asteroids and space-meat bits.

The signs read, 'Speed limit: light years ahead,'
But who's counting? Just follow Fred!
He's a space cat on a scooter ride,
With a helmet on, he'll be our guide.

Laughter echoes through the starlit ways,
Where even black holes are just silly bays.
In this cosmic realm where all is bright,
We cruise for fun, until the day turns to night.

Parallel Pathways

Two paths diverge in a quantum tale,
One might lead you to the moon or a whale.
With a wink and a giggle, take your pick,
In the multiverse, time's just a trick.

On one side, there's tea with a toad,
On the other, rides on a meteor road.
Jump through dimensions, flip like a coin,
In this wild realm, all joys you'll join.

Interstellar ducks quack in a row,
Waddling past stars that glimmer and glow.
Each parallel turn twists the same way,
Just watch out for the rifts in the play.

With friends on each side, why not explore?
In this funny world, there's always more.
Take a jump and embrace the odd,
In parallel pathways, we laugh and trod.

Astral Adventures

Pack your bags with stardust and dreams,
Ready for laughter and comical themes.
We'll surf the waves of the galactic sea,
With rubber ducks and a cup of tea.

Meeting creatures with five-pointed hats,
Dancing with space squirrels and cosmic rats.
We navigate comets like boardwalks of light,
In this outlandish realm, what a sight!

We'll skip on stars and play hide and seek,
With moonbeams as bridges, it's all unique.
A tickle fight in the rings of a star,
Who knew that space could be this bizarre?

As we bounce through galaxies, full of cheer,
We'll laugh with the cosmos, never a fear.
Adventure awaits in this vast drifty sea,
With funny quirks, oh, come ride with me!

Fluctuations of Fate

I tripped on a cosmic plan,
Fell through dimensions, oh what a fan!
Saw a cat with a bowtie, quite grand,
Offered me tea, as we both stand.

A fish on a skateboard zipped past,
Said, "This isn't built to last!"
But I just laughed, and danced away,
Chasing photons, come what may.

A chicken crossed to the other side,
Said, "I wanted to take a ride!"
With space dust stuck upon its beak,
It winked at me with a galaxy streak.

Fate's a jester playing tricks,
Knocking on doors with ghostly clicks.
I'll ride this wave of chaos spun,
With starry socks, just for fun!

Beyond the Veil of Stars

They say there's gold where meteors fall,
I found a sock and gave it a call.
A hoot from the void, oh what a treat,
Dancing comets, got two left feet.

A raccoon in space with a shiny tin,
Proclaimed, "Join my band, let's begin!"
They strummed on the strings of cosmic rays,
While asteroids tapped out silly plays.

Oh look, a spaceship made out of cheese,
It flew in circles with graceful ease.
A moonbeam chef cooked up a delight,
With stardust sprinkles, what a sight!

Through portals that giggle and sneeze,
I wander with laughter, if you please.
Beyond the veil where the silly bloom,
I'll dance 'til I land in my living room!

Rift Reveries

In a crack in the sky, dreams take a tow,
Sailing with pirates who don't even row.
They're juggling stars like they're in a show,
With laughter echoing from toe to toe.

A gnome in a rocket, in pajamas so bright,
Shouted, "To infinity, hold on tight!"
But his rocket was more like a paper plane,
As we sailed through the giggles and rain.

An octopus painted in polka dots,
Drinks fizzy drinks from crystal pots.
It waltzed with a comet, so far and wide,
Together they laughed and swayed with pride.

So here I float in this rift of dreams,
Chasing the laughter, hearing the beams.
We're snickers and snorts, cosmic in play,
In reveries vast where the funny stay!

Universe Untamed

In the wild where the quarks like to dance,
I found a lion who offered a chance.
He wore funky glasses, said, "Come explore!"
So together we pranced, seeking out more.

Through galaxies swirled like a giant soup,
A walrus with sunglasses joined our troop.
He played the accordion, what a delight,
As meteors twinkled, twirling in flight.

A squirrel in space with a big fluff tail,
Sold acorn cookies that never go stale.
The snacks were cosmic, with sprinkles of fun,
And we laughed at the chaos, oh how we run!

So let's ride this weird and wild stream,
With giggles and wonders, how we beam!
The universe howls with a chuckle and twist,
In this vast expanse of a magical list!

Enigmatic Frontiers

I packed my snacks and took a leap,
Into the unknown, where secrets creep.
With a wink and a nod, I hit the gas,
Who knew the cosmos would be such a blast?

Planets twirl like dizzy kids,
While space cats dance, wearing lids.
Floating spheres of jelly beans,
Life's a circus; watch the scenes!

Aliens wave, they throw confetti,
I'm the oddball—unwilling yet ready.
I slip on a space shoe, what a style!
In this wild ride, I can only smile.

Gravity's out; my bagel's lost,
In search of the bagel, that's the cost.
Yet with each twist and unexpected turn,
I find new treasures in my yearn.

Journeying Through the Ether

Off I zoom in my trusty pod,
Dodging asteroids—oh, how I applaud!
The nachos are slipping, what a delight,
Floating around in this cosmic sight.

Stars are giggling, they're in on the joke,
A meteor's dancing, with a spark and a poke.
I join in the fun, can't miss this chance,
In this wild universe, I'm learning to dance.

Planets wearing hats, what a sight to behold,
They giggle and smile, or so they're told.
Getting lost in their laughter, my compass goes mute,
The secret of space? It's rarely astute!

Celestial highways with no speed limit,
In my spaceship, I'm far from timid.
With snacks in hand, I take a wild flight,
Through the ether I soar, oh what a night!

Fractals of Fate

In a fractal whirl, the patterns surprise,
With each twist and turn, I witness the skies.
The universe chuckles, it's quite a show,
Every chance taken leads where I don't know.

Galaxies spinning in colors so bright,
Cosmic confetti that fills up my sight.
I trip on the starlight, oops—what a slip!
End up on a comet, who's offering a sip?

Dimensions undulate, in laughter we bask,
Inquiring minds, it's a curious task.
Plotting a path through this giggling maze,
Every detour, a laugh-filled phase.

I tip my hat to fate's silly tricks,
Crafting adventures from cosmic flicks.
So let's ride the laughter, embrace the play,
In this universe, joy's come what may!

The Allure of Celestial Shores

Surfing the stars on cosmic waves,
Building sandcastles that spacetime saves.
With cosmic sunscreen slathered on thick,
I order a drink that's frozen, not quick.

The shore glimmers with stardust fine,
While aliens sip on their space-time wine.
I join in their banter, we laugh and we jest,
An intergalactic beach day is always the best.

Under a sun that dances with flair,
I realized my towel's stuck in mid-air.
Chasing flapping clothes, what a funny sight,
With joy in my heart, I embrace the night.

As waves of laughter crash on the sand,
I gather new friends from every land.
In this cosmic resort, where fun is at core,
With joy as my guide, I'm forever wanting more!

Tunnels to Tomorrow

In a tube that glows and sways,
I lost my lunch on the way.
Pasta swirled in cosmic dance,
Oh, what a wild, wobbly chance!

Riding light like a joyous kite,
I giggle at the speed of light.
Cats and cows float past my head,
I'm not quite sure if I'm still bread.

A flying toaster zips on by,
Should I wave or just comply?
In this lane of snack-filled bliss,
Every detour tastes like a kiss!

Gravity? That's just a prank,
Jumping high in my timey bank.
Tomorrow's meals come with delight,
Just watch out for that cheese that bites!

Shadows of Distant Realms

In a realm where shadows creep,
I found a frog that loves to leap.
He offered me a sip of goo,
I said, "No thanks, but how 'bout you?"

Dancing moons in crazy shades,
Play hopscotch with the neon glades.
A pickle plays the lute with flair,
As I twirl without a care.

Chasing shadows in a twist,
Glitter monsters can't resist.
They tap dance on my silly hat,
I'm giggling here, how 'bout that?

With every laugh, the darkness fades,
An octopus does pirouettes in spades.
In this strange and silly scene,
I grip my sandwich, feeling keen!

The Traveler's Paradox

A paradox in every way,
I lost my legs, but hey, hooray!
Wheels for days and a grin so wide,
I roll through time like a joyride.

Met a doppelganger in a hat,
He stole my sandwich, just like that!
We laughed it off, then traded fries,
Toasted futures in starry skies.

Confused my schedule, lost my mind,
I caught a ride on a cloud-shaped grind.
With candy rains and chocolate streams,
Future me—what a wild dream!

But how do I get back, you ask?
Through giggles, leads—an easy task!
In between the now and then,
I found a friend; let's do this again!

Whispers Across Dimensions

In a realm where whispers giggle,
I overheard a sound that wiggled.
A talking chair just spilled the tea,
It said, "Dance like nobody's free!"

Fish in suits strolled by with flair,
Dressed so sharp, I thought, "That's rare!"
Their bow ties flapped like wings in flight,
As I spun round, what a sight!

I chased a bubble that knew my name,
It popped and splashed; oh, what a game!
With every laugh, the stars aligned,
In this dimension, I'm undefined.

So here's the secret, take it far,
Life's a dance with a twinkling star.
Embrace the giggle, the joy, the thrill,
In whispers, the universe always will!

Atmospheric Amblings

In a rocket made of cheese,
We zoom past stars with ease,
Galaxies wave with a grin,
As we stick our heads out to spin.

Meteors try to play a game,
Yet they're just too shy for fame,
As comets hiccup on the go,
Saying, "What's the rush? Enjoy the show!"

With googly eyes on every sun,
We dance and laugh, it's all in fun,
Jupiter's storms join in the cheer,
While Saturn gives a flashy rear.

Floating space donuts come our way,
We munch and drift, it's quite the play,
In an orbit made of giggle beams,
We live among our cosmic dreams.

The Lure of the Unknown

A sign says 'Enter—if you dare!'
We snicker and run through the air,
Past portals that tickle and tease,
Into realms where socks dance with ease.

A planet made of jellybeans,
And rivers of chocolatey streams,
Where aliens have petting zoos,
With fuzzy creatures that enjoy blues.

Platypuses play hopscotch on Mars,
While we ride bicycles made of stars,
Every spin brings a cosmic surprise,
A trip where laughter never dies.

So grab your hat, it's time to roam,
In the land where whimsies call home,
Adventure's a lighthearted game,
In worlds where everyone knows your name.

Celestial Cartographers

With maps made of silly swirls,
We chart the laughs and giggles of worlds,
Each mark a giggle, each line a jest,
In the fabric of time, we find the best.

Stars are just dots wearing crowns,
Spinning yarns where nothing drowns,
Black holes open to sing a tune,
As we dance under the light of the moon.

Comets take selfies, a cosmic spree,
Replaying moments for you and me,
We scribble on clouds and draw in space,
Every sketch brings a smiling face.

Navigating through the silly skies,
Where laughter reigns and fun never dies,
Celestial maps, both bright and bold,
Lead to adventures waiting to unfold.

Beyond the Cosmic Canvas

Painted skies with splashes of cheer,
We dip our brushes, oh so near,
Each star a dot, each planet a brush,
Creating chaos with cosmic hush.

A canvas that giggles, swirls and bends,
Where creativity never ends,
With paint that glows in every hue,
We splash on joy, both old and new.

Brush strokes that dance like silly feet,
As we juggle colors in the heat,
The galaxies join our happy quest,
In this art where we are truly blessed.

So let's paint together, you and I,
In the laughter echoing on high,
Beyond the canvas, we'll forever glide,
In a universe where fun will abide.

Lightyear Leap

In a spaceship with googly eyes,
We blast through stars and rubber flies.
Pizza floats in zero G,
As we race the moon, just wait and see!

A comet sneezes, bright and loud,
We giggle under a galactic cloud.
Space squirrels visit, wearing hats,
While dancing to the tunes of spacey chats.

The aliens wave with jelly beans,
As we skateboard on cosmic streams.
Learning to parallel park on Mars,
While taking selfies with Venusian stars!

Rocket boosters filled with fizz,
We zoom past time – oh what a whiz!
Our laughter echoes in the void,
In this lightyear leap, we're overjoyed!

Nebula Navigators

We don our hats of sparkling dust,
In a nebula, we find our trust.
Guided by a cat with a map,
We hop through clouds in a cheerful flap!

Galactic markets sell space fudge,
Where starfish barter and time does budge.
We try to cook with cosmic rays,
And end up with goo on all our trays!

The black holes laugh, they think it's fate,
As we juggle moons and argue about cake.
With every twist and turn we find,
A cosmic giggle shared by all humankind.

Shooting stars race, oh what a sight,
We cheer and tumble through day and night.
Navigators of the vibrant hue,
In this nebula, we always renew!

Quantum Journeys

Riding beams of light that bend,
We quantum jump around the bend.
A frog in space looks awfully grand,
As we twist and turn in a marching band!

Particles dancing in a waltz,
We choose our paths as luck exalts.
With socks that shimmer and shoes that beep,
We take giant leaps, oh what a sweep!

A time machine that's shaped like cheese,
Whisk us away if you please!
Through fractals of giggles, we spin and fly,
As bubbles giggle and stars keep nigh.

Tick-tock goes our silly clock,
With calendars made of potato rock.
In quantum realms where fun won't cease,
We dance with physics, a quirky feast!

Celestial Wanderers

With candy craters and jelly bean streams,
We wander through the land of dreams.
Rocket shoes that bounce and sway,
Make each day a giggling ballet!

Caught in a whirlwind of glittering haze,
The suns do a dance, in cosmic maze.
A starry parade of dancing cats,
With tutus and bonnets, imagine that!

We ride on meteors, slip and slide,
Through Saturn's rings, we gleefully glide.
With stardust smoothies and quasar fries,
Every meal brings a new surprise!

In this realm of whimsical delight,
We twirl 'neath the moons, oh what a sight.
Celestial beings join the fun,
In this endless party, we've just begun!

Gravity of Longing

When I jump, I float like cheese,
Chasing stars that tickle my knees.
Socks on comets, giggles galore,
All this longing, I can ignore.

A starry sandwich, I take a bite,
The universe winks, oh what a sight!
Floating past planets, I'll take a stroll,
Who knew space was such a rock-n-roll?

Echoes in the Beyond

Bouncing off quasars, I hear them laugh,
A cosmic dance with a polka giraffe.
Meteors sing songs in silly tones,
Echoes of laughter between the big stones.

I asked a black hole for a good joke,
It said, 'I've got one, but it's too smoke!'
Dancing through stardust, tickle my spine,
Space is a circus, and it's all mine!

Celestial Drift

Floating on clouds, I sip starry tea,
Caffeine from Pluto flows wild and free.
Jupiter's belly laughs at my dreams,
While Saturn spins yarns of cosmic schemes.

Asteroids tap dance, what a delight,
In the silence of space, they twirl at night.
Galaxies wink as I drift on by,
In this twilight laughter, I'll never die.

Maps of Forgotten Dreams

I once drew a map where the stars all wink,
The ink was stardust in shades of pink.
Chasing my dreams on a dandy old kite,
Lost in the cosmos, it feels just right.

Each line a giggle, each dot a smile,
Navigating space with undeniable style.
Plans to catch comets, with cupcakes too,
In the universe's sketch, I made a zoo.

Hyperdrive Horizons

Zooming through the cosmic lanes,
With snacks that float like rolling trains.
I spilled my drink, it's turned to gas,
Why did I think this ride would last?

Planets pass like blurs on screens,
Chasing space cats and alien beans.
I tripped on stardust, fell on Mars,
Now I'm dating a guy from the stars!

Galactic karaoke, what a sight,
Singing with aliens deep in the night.
They don't mind if I miss a note,
As long as I dance in my shiny coat!

Jumping through rings that spin and play,
With a rubber duck that's here to stay.
In this crazy ride, all's a thrill,
Warped to laughter, I'll never chill!

Space-time Strolls

Strolling through the fabric of space,
Wobbly feet in this endless race.
I bumped a comet, it gave a laugh,
Said it was just my recent gaffe!

Dancing on planets made of cheese,
While dodging meteors with the greatest of ease.
A cosmic chase with a flailing arm,
The universe laughs; I'm full of charm!

Twisting through timelines like silly string,
A time-traveling fool, oh the joy I bring!
I accidentally dated my grandpa, oh dear,
But he showed me space-flavored root beer!

We giggle and glide, no need to hurry,
Though past and present can be blurry.
With each step, the stars bend low,
In this belly laugh of cosmic flow!

The Celestial Compass

My compass points in circles wide,
Got lost in Venus, just can't hide.
It spins and whirls; I grab my hat,
I'm not a twinkling star, but a fluffed-up cat!

Navigating chaos in a tangled web,
With a guide that's a space-faring celeb.
They laugh and point as I trip and sway,
Through asteroid fields, we play all day!

Orbits are just a game of tag,
Dodging black holes, trying not to lag.
With laughter ringing through the dark,
I tickle a comet; it leaves a spark!

Finding my way, I miss the signs,
Each rib-tickling twirl, a gobbler of vines.
The stars applaud my comedic flair,
In this cosmic dance without a care!

Beyond the Starscape

Beyond the stars where laughter gleams,
I ride on photons, gliding on beams.
A universe where chuckles reign,
Sailing on giggles — oh, it's insane!

Floating past planets in silly hats,
Hitchhiking with space-faring spats.
I offered a moon a cup of tea,
It threw a party; oh, what glee!

Bursting in laughter at a supernova,
They say it's just physics, but I'm a trover.
Juggling asteroids like they're beach balls,
While my spaceship bounces off cosmic walls!

Twinkling stars, come join the fun,
In this party where we run and run.
Beyond the stars with silly delight,
In a universe where doubting's polite!

Scenic Slipstream

In a twisty tunnel, I took flight,
My snack pack floating, what a sight!
Space cats grinning, chasing my tail,
Lost my sandwich, oh, this can't fail!

Einstein's ghost, he gave a wink,
Sipped on stardust, had a drink.
Tickled by comets, I twirled around,
Singing with aliens, quite profound!

Twirling on beams of light, I soared,
Riding giggles, never bored.
Gravity's silly dance made me sway,
Here in the slipstream, I love to play!

In this zany ride, I lost my shoes,
Stomped on star clusters, sang blues.
Juggling moons with a cheerful grin,
Who knew the cosmos could be such a win!

Time's Tapestry

Sailing through ages, what a ride,
Sedans of the past, they glide!
T-Rex waved, wearing a hat,
Sent me a selfie, imagine that!

Goblins in togas, dancing a jig,
"Hey, dude!" they yell, mischief so big.
Futuristic poodles trim and neat,
Brought me a burger, oh, what a treat!

Tick-tock, I tried to fix the clock,
But wound up dancing a timey-wok.
Chronicles folded like creased-up maps,
Flipping through timelines, oh, what a lapse!

Every tick echoes, laughter's theme,
In this fabric of time where we dream.
Spilling for pudding, a history stew,
Forever in stitches, me and you!

Odyssey Through the Unknown

Packed my bag for a silly spree,
Disco balls in space, just me!
Zigzagging planets, curving so tight,
Mr. Moon gave me a goofy fright.

Neon fish zooming, they play my tune,
Pretend I'm a rock star, howling at noon.
Planets throw parties, cake in the air,
Messy confetti, floating everywhere!

Blasted by meteor, I'm tossed like a ball,
Landed in jelly on Saturn's hall.
Laughed with a robot, shared a strong brew,
Deciding that existentialism's nothing new.

Riding the comets, I sing "Woo-hoo!"
Who knew the stars could dance like we do?
Running with giants in neon shoes,
Adventures beyond, who could refuse?

Stellar Vagabonds

Sailing in stardust, what a thrill,
My cosmic cruise, let's pay the bill!
Bumping into giants, we shared some pie,
"Lost my spaceship!" I shouted, oh my!

Puppies in spacesuits, barking for treats,
Chasing around on zero-gravity streets.
Distant worlds waving, they all wore shades,
Join me, they joked, "It's fun like charades!"

Falling through galaxies with a splat,
Fell into Martian fields, how about that?
Singing silly songs beneath shooting stars,
Writing a hit, look out for our bars!

Galloping comets and dancing moons,
Cosmic glitches and celestial tunes.
Together as vagabonds, we hoot and sway,
Cartwheeling through the cosmos, hooray!

Galaxy Gallivanting

I packed my bags to roam the skies,
With fluffy clouds and pizza pies.
I tripped on stars, they giggled loud,
As I floated past a disco cloud.

A comet winked, a moon did dance,
I joined their tune, oh what a chance!
With neon lights and candy bars,
I spun around the distant stars.

Dimensions Untold

I opened doors to worlds unknown,
Where jellybeans sat on a throne.
I asked for snacks, they passed me pie,
A talking cat taught me to fly.

I sneezed and fell through a purple wall,
Landed in a land where gravity's small.
Elastic trees with stretchy leaves,
Invited me for tea, what a tease!

Starlit Escapades

I jumped on beams of silver light,
Flew with fairies, oh what a sight!
We played hide and seek in cosmic dust,
With stardust giggles, in fun we trust.

Met aliens who danced on the moon,
In pajamas, singing their silly tune.
They served me snacks made from space cheese,
And all I felt was pure, simple ease.

Temporal Travels

I hopped in time, like skipping rope,
Met dinosaurs who tried to yelp hope.
We shared a laugh, played hopscotch bad,
With T-Rex arms, oh how they had!

I zapped to future, where robots cook,
But they burned toast, oh what a hook!
They offered me a circuit pie,
I took a bite, and then I cried!

The Lattice of Space-time

In a twist of space and time,
I found my socks lost, oh so sublime.
Floating past some cheese and wine,
I chuckled, what an intergalactic crime!

Navigating cosmic snacks and glee,
I tripped over a star, can't you see?
A comet offered me a cup of tea,
Amidst the stars, I felt so carefree.

Bouncing past planets with a giggly bounce,
Where gravity took a silly pounce.
I danced on Saturn's rings, a light trounce,
Chased by an alien cat with a frown!

From black holes to stardust, all in a whir,
Lost in the cosmic, I laugh with a blur.
I'll take the next portal, forget the sir,
In this tangled web, the fun is a spur!

Odyssey of the Unexplored

On a ship made of candy, I set my sails,
With marshmallow crew and jellybean trails.
We voyaged through space, where nothing pales,
Zipping past giants with gummy snail tales!

Dodging asteroids with my sticky wit,
Cracking jokes in the cosmic split.
Found a planet where the candy bars sit,
But the chocolate was sticky; I couldn't commit!

With every twist, my journey unfolds,
I exchanged giggles, my laughter behold!
Counted comets like priceless gold,
A treasure of silliness, forever bold.

Waves of laughter across the vast night,
Made friends with robots who danced without fright.
As we drifted in stardust, everything felt right,
In this realm of fun, I took flight!

Interstellar Reveries

As I traveled through pixels, lightyears away,
I traded my worries for stardust of play.
Bouncing on meteors, in bright array,
My interstellar dreams took me astray!

An octopus wore space boots and twirled,
While unicorns giggled, their manes all unfurled.
We danced with the planets, our laughter hurled,
A cosmic ballet, where wonders unfurled.

With a wink from a nova, I grinned with glee,
Scribbled my thoughts in the dark cosmic sea.
Found a trampoline made of space debris,
Jumped high into laughter, oh, what a spree!

In the zany bubble of the universe bright,
I spun tales of joy with pure delight.
In the echoes of laughter, I took flight,
Every star a giggle, most out of sight!

Rifts of Exploration

Through rifts and giggles, I leaped with a cheer,
Encountered strange creatures with snacks near.
Munching on starlight, oh, sweet souvenir,
In the realms of nonsense, there's nothing to fear!

A turtle in space wore a tutu so grand,
And tossed around moons like they were in hand.
With each bouncing joke, we made quite a band,
Our laughter echoed like an orchestra's stand.

Riding the beams of a rainbow-lit bridge,
Over planets that glimmered, we danced in a ridge.
Met a dancing black hole doing a jig,
As time ticked funny, like a cosmic big!

Banana-flavored comets shot by with flair,
While giggles of stardust filled up the air.
In this colorful swirl, joy was laid bare,
Exploring the cosmos, without a care!

Constellation Dares

Twinkle toes on a starry race,
Dodging comets in a cosmic chase.
Aliens laughing, what a sight,
While I trip over asteroids at night.

Galactic games in a black hole's grip,
I tried to moonwalk, ended in a flip.
Jupiter's belly laughs, oh so round,
As Saturn sings with its ringed sound.

Astral Abodes

Living on Mars? I've packed my snacks,
But no one warned me about the cracks.
I tried to plant my daisies in dust,
They winked at me and said, 'We must!'

Venus holds a saucer of tea,
But talked to me like I was a flea.
Neptune's storms gave me quite a fright,
I asked for a shower, got a light fight.

Tidal Shifts of Space

Riding waves of cosmic brine,
Surfing stardust, feeling fine.
The moon's my coach with a cheeky grin,
Says, 'You'll wipe out, but you can always spin!'

Galaxies dance in an endless flow,
While I'm clumsy like a space-time show.
Gravity giggles as I jump high,
Crashing down—oh my, oh my!

Cosmic Curiosities

I found a star wearing mismatched shoes,
Asked if it's a fashion or just to amuse?
Planets spun tales like an old granddad,
While meteors tossed popcorn, it's not so bad!

Dancing with quasars, doing the twist,
With a black hole leading, I couldn't resist.
A laugh in the void, oh what a delight,
In this celestial carnival, everything feels right.

Nomads of the Nebula

In shiny ships we zoom and sway,
Chasing stars that dance and play.
With snacks in hand and tunes so bright,
We giggle through the cosmic night.

Our maps are drawn in jelly signs,
While aliens sip on fizzy wines.
We swap our tales with goofy grins,
As gravity gives in to our spins.

Through colors wild and giggles loud,
We hug the comets, feeling proud.
With each jump, new friends we meet,
In this vast space that can't be beat.

So join our flight, bring your own hats,
And let's toast to cosmic spats.
In our nebula, laughter rings,
Floating with the weirdest things.

Floating in Frequencies

We slide on beams of funky light,
With boombox bass that feels just right.
A cosmic DJ spins a tune,
While dancing moons hum a cartoon.

Twirling in a spiral waltz,
Our gravity's just a cute false jolt.
We chat with clouds, they know the scoop,
On galactic gossip and gummy soup.

Echoes bounce from star to star,
As we ride waves and sip bizarre.
With giggles tickling stardust air,
We show our moves without a care.

So tune in close and catch the wave,
In frequency realms where we are brave.
The universe knows how to have fun,
As we unite and become one.

Quantum Quest

In realms where particles play hide and seek,
We leap dimensions, feeling unique.
With every step, a joke to tell,
As Schrödinger's cat rings a bell.

We laugh at time's tangled threads,
As spacetime hops on our funny beds.
Oh, join us now, we're feeling bold,
In waves of laughter, our stories unfold.

We tickle quarks and tease the rays,
Sharing tales of cosmic ballets.
With each new leap, the fun just grows,
As silly science forever flows.

So pack your quirks and hop along,
In this strange dance, we all belong.
For every particle needs a jest,
In this adventure, we're truly blessed.

Ethereal Expeditions

Through misty realms where giggles spin,
We float on dreams, collecting wins.
With sparkly maps in hand we roam,
To find the quirkiest of home.

Our leader's just a penguin's hat,
Which tells us tales of cosmic Pat.
We ride on clouds of cotton candy,
In this wild quest that's pure and dandy.

With unicorns and starry hugs,
We sip on drinks from cosmic mugs.
We'll forge ahead with silly hearts,
In this grand journey where laughter starts.

So take a step and let's embark,
On wild quests that leave a mark.
For in this realm of twists and turns,
The joy of space forever burns.

Cosmic Veins of Desire

In the galaxy's quick snack bar,
A burger flies fast, oh so bizarre.
Jupiter's fries are quite a catch,
But in Saturn's ring, ketchup's a sketch.

My spaceship's stuck in a cosmic jam,
Traffic's no joke, I swear, oh fam!
Shooting stars zoom past with a wink,
"Is that a comet?" I stop to think.

Planets are dancing in disarray,
Mercury claims he's on a diet today.
Pluto rolls eyes, says "I'm still a star,"
And Mars giggles hard, "You're just too far!"

Yet among the fun on interstellar roads,
It's hard to find snacks that aren't just codes.
So I'll munch on light rays, with glee I toast,
To the cosmic cravings of this silly host!

Through the Fabric of Infinity

A sock appeared in the void of space,
Did it travel here from an alien place?
I pulled on threads of a never-ending yarn,
Knitted a scarf that looked quite un-charmed.

Galaxies tumble like clumsy fools,
Trying to follow their own set of rules.
Time takes a break for a fateful laugh,
As quarks play hopscotch on the cosmic path.

With every twist, a giggle unfolds,
The universe sneezes, it's too bright, too bold!
"Bless you!" I shout to the stars all around,
In this woven joke, joy's found unbound.

Planets wear hats that are quite out of style,
Dancing through echoes, oh what a while!
In the fabric of dreams, the stitches shake,
Stitching weird tales that the cosmos make.

Portals to the Unseen

I found a door in my backyard's hedge,
Who knew the view would make me pledge?
To skip through dimensions, take a quick peek,
To an alternate world that's entirely bleak.

In a land where cows jump and fly,
I asked them, "What's the secret to high?"
They just moo'd and floated with ease,
As I scribbled notes on intergalactic cheese.

Next, I danced with a cat in a hat,
Who claimed that the moon was his latest spat.
"Don't take it personal," he slyly grinned,
"Just hop through this portal, where fun is twinned!"

Yet home calls me back with its warm embrace,
So I'll stash my notes and quicken my pace.
To portals unseen, I'll bid my goodbye,
While plotting new journeys through the old sky!

Starbound Journeys

With a rocket made from soda cans,
I'm zooming through space with my feline fans.
Each star we pass just winks and glows,
"Where to next?" my adventurous nose knows.

At the edge of the universe, I spill my drink,
My cat just shrugs, "We'll figure, don't blink!"
Each droplet's a universe, hidden and bright,
We're surfing on stardust, that's our flight!

Uranus had a joke that took ages to tell,
"Why can't planets keep secrets so well?"
I laughed so hard, I nearly slipped,
My rocket went spinning, it flipped and flipped!

But giggles abound, through the cosmos we glide,
With felines and fizz, let's dance in the tide.
Starbound journeys, oh what a run,
In a universe of laughter, we'll have our fun!

Starry Wanderlust Elegy

In a ship made of pizza, I sail the night,
Chasing a comet, what a silly sight.
Jellybean planets orbit the cheese,
And I munch on stardust, quite at ease.

Dancing with aliens in bright tutus,
They teach me their dance, it's one big ruse.
Eating space muffins, they say they're great,
But they taste like the remnants of a long-lost date.

My GPS is a cat, it's always lost,
It takes me on voyages, no matter the cost.
Yet somehow I smile, in this cosmic spree,
Who knew that space travel could be so cheesy?

So here's to the journeys, ridiculous and wide,
With intergalactic giggles, I'll ride the tide.
Though my ship's made of candy, I'll never be sad,
For the jokes of the cosmos are the best I've had!

Expedition to the Great Beyond

Packed my bag with glitter and a spoon,
Off to explore the funky side of the moon.
Every crater's a party, a disco in space,
With robots doing the hustle, what a hilarious place!

I met a green creature with ten million eyes,
It said, "Want to see my pet meteor flies?"
We launched them in orbits, they glimmer and spark,
But they crashed into comets—oh boy, what a lark!

Doodling with starlight, creating a mess,
The galaxy's my canvas, oh what a success!
I painted with laughter and brushed with pure glee,
In this grand expedition, I'm wild and free.

So raise your juice boxes, let's toast to the stars,
Where the weirdness is plenty with aliens in cars.
In this chase through the cosmos where nothing's too far,
Every hiccup's a giggle—what a laugh, how bizarre!

Portal Pursuits

I entered a portal made of bubblegum,
Sliced through dimensions, oh what a hum!
I landed in movies—Hollywood roared,
Chased by dinosaurs, I was totally floored!

With popcorn for planets and soda for stars,
I watched superheroes battle in fancy cars.
Where unicorns fly and ninjas eat pie,
The universe laughs as reality goes sly.

A time-traveling toaster popped up with a grin,
"Let's toast to the ages, where do we begin?"
We blasted through time, to the age of the fish,
Where they danced to the tunes of the great, silly swish.

In this vortex of laughter, I can't help but cheer,
Each twist in the cosmos brings giggles near here.
So grab your odd socks, for strange journeys await,
In portals of whimsy, we'll celebrate fate!

Interstellar Sojourn

Through fields of confetti, I drift and I sway,
Dancing on asteroids, what a magical play.
With my silicone armadillo named Dave,
We spin in the nebula, oh how we rave!

I swam with the fish in the vast cosmic sea,
They wore little goggles; their laughter was free.
Our bubbles were filled with jokes and delight,
As we zoomed through the stardust, what an odd sight!

A moon made of chocolate, oh what a treat,
I baked a nice cake for the aliens to eat.
But they mixed up the recipe, oh what a crime,
They served it with sprinkles and said it's sublime.

So here's to our travels, both silly and bright,
In the cosmos we wander, with spirits of light.
A journey of chuckles, of dreams and of fun,
In the realm of stars, we'll never be done!

The Journey Beyond

I packed my bags with snacks and dreams,
A ticket to nowhere, or so it seems.
My cat's in charge, she's flying the ship,
Paw on the joystick, we're ready to skip.

The stars are winking, what a sight!
I asked a comet to join for a bite.
It brought a friend, a dancing asteroid,
Said, "Let's party hard, you won't be bored!"

We looped 'round planets, each one a tease,
Giggled with aliens—guests at the knees.
They offered me pie, of a flavor unknown,
Said, "Try it, my friend, you'll feel right at home!"

As the trip winds down, I can feel my cheer,
But my cat's snoring loud—uh-oh, this could stear!
I wave goodbye to the glittering night,
Next stop is Earth, for a nap, not a flight!

Echoes of the Expanse

In a vacuum, I shouted, "Hello, is there life?"
A distant echo replied with some strife.
"Can't understand you, I've misplaced my ear!"
My own silly laugh was all that I'd hear.

I danced with stardust, got lost on a sun,
Thought I could surf, but it wasn't that fun.
Fell through a nebula, swirled through the haze,
Came out with glitter—got new style praise!

My spaceship's a mess—what a sight to behold,
Covered in donuts, they're crispy and bold!
The galaxy's scheming a cosmic delight,
With desserts that mock, is it cake or is it light?

I buzzed with pulsars, each twinkling their glee,
Yet each chat got messy—spilled sugary tea.
Stars rolled with laughter, and black holes twirled tight,
Bound for the next void—oh, what a great night!

The Call of the Cosmos

Under the stars, I heard a sweet tune,
A calling from Saturn—a jazzy balloon.
The rings they were twinkling, in sassy parade,
Inviting this dreamer to join in their charade.

A rocketship party, what a silly scenes!
Cow aliens danced like they got no routines.
I spilled my drink on a three-headed dog,
Laughed as he stared, looking like a fog.

The Milky Way wrapped us in whimsical style,
Jupiter chuckled; he's got quite the smile.
I tried on a comet, it fit like a glove,
Flying through space, all the alien love.

But as all good things must come to their end,
I waved to the stars, my joyous best friend.
Back to my earth, with a grin on my face,
Until the next party in our wild space race!

Explorers of the Unseen

We set off for places where no one has been,
With snacks in our pockets, we grinned like a fiend.
A pirate ship floated, all covered in goo,
Turns out, it's just lunch—glistening stew!

We wobbled through time on our silly space bikes,
Buzzing through wormholes, like cosmic tykes.
"What's that shiny thing?" I yelled with delight,
Just a satellite leading the way, what a sight!

Met beings with tentacles, each wore a hat,
"Join us for tea!" They said, "Have a chat!"
I spilled my whole milk on a green lunchbox,
Laughed as they danced, two-headed and socks!

The universe giggled; we reached for the stars,
But tripped on a meteor, flew up—oh, the bars!
And as we fell home, laughter roared from above,
For there's joy in each journey, and endless love.

Infinite Horizons

I packed my bag, a snack in hand,
To explore the stars, oh isn't that grand!
A strange machine sat in my yard,
I hopped inside, it didn't seem hard.

Off I zoomed in a giddy flight,
Past quirks of space that danced with light.
A purple cow floated by my side,
We mooed at planets, oh what a ride!

I dodged a comet, then slipped on a ring,
A joke about gravity made me laugh and sing.
Stars wiggled their toes, what a sight to behold,
This cosmic escapade was a joy to unfold!

With each new twist, my giggles grew loud,
Chasing constellations, I felt so proud.
I landed back home with a bounce and a spin,
I laughed to myself, oh where to begin!

Enigmatic Expanses

In the depths of space, I found a door,
It squeaked like a cat, oh what a bore!
I turned the knob, and entered a realm,
Where ducks wore coats and owls did helm.

With a wave from a fish in a top hat bright,
I strolled through clouds that sparkled at night.
I rode on a snail that moved at a crawl,
But the view from its shell was the best of all!

I danced with the stars, they twirled in surprise,
As I learned the moon could do the cha-cha so wise.
I knocked on a black hole, but it wouldn't reply,
It simply pulled me, and oh my, oh my!

When I zipped back to Earth with a flip and a flop,
I glanced at my watch—it'd skipped a whole crop!
I laughed at the chaos, the silliness too,
What a wild jaunt, oh, if only you knew!

Dreamscapes of the Universe

In dreamlike realms, I took a ride,
On a bubble of laughter, not a care inside.
A unicorn popped out with glittering flair,
While a cactus sang songs in the cosmic air.

I tripped over stardust and danced on a ray,
Met a wizard who claimed he lost his bouquet.
He juggled some planets, they fell, oh dear,
I cracked up so hard, I rolled on my sphere!

With giggles that echoed through nebulous light,
I chatted with comets, all shiny and bright.
A jellybean stole the show with its glee,
It bounced off the sun, then winked at me.

Home I returned with giggles galore,
Who knew space travel could offer such score?
With dreams of the universe swirling with fun,
I smiled at the magic this journey had spun!

The Allure of Altitudes

I climbed to the peak of a rainbow high,
Where clouds wore hats, and penguins would fly.
With giggles and grins, we slid down the hue,
To meet with a critter, a spotty kangaroo.

He offered me snacks from a suitcase well packed,
With jelly and jellybeans, oh weren't we racked!
We played hide and seek among aspen trees,
Laughter erupted with every cool breeze.

A squirrel in goggles zoomed past on a bike,
As we cheered him on with a jolly old strike.
Chasing our shadows, we floated and twirled,
Who knew such whimsy could lighten the world?

When twilight draped stars like a shimmering quilt,
I whispered my secrets, the joy that I felt.
Returning from heights with a heart full of cheer,
Life's greatest adventures are always so near!

Timeless Trails

In cosmic boots, we stomp and stomp,
Chasing stars, a merry romp.
What's that smell? Is it space stew?
Dinner's served, it's moonlight goo!

Round the bend, we trip and slide,
Through glitter trails, we laugh and glide.
Oh dear, I think I lost my shoe,
Guess it's now a satellite too!

Juggling comets, what a show!
Twirling planets, to and fro.
A wink from Mars, a giggle from Venus,
This cosmic circus is beyond genius!

Racing light, we zip and zoom,
Across the void, we make our room.
With every twist, a funny twist,
A cosmic joke we can't resist!

Wandering Within the Void

I drift through space with glee and flair,
Counting stars beyond compare.
But where's my snack? Did I forget?
Galactic chips, oh, what a bet!

Floating high on laughter's beam,
In this vast, whimsical dream.
A dance with dust, the giggles rise,
Who knew voids came with such surprise?

Met a photon, in shades of blue,
It winked at me and then it flew.
"Hey buddy, want to race me now?"
I chuckled back, "You're on, I vow!"

In the darkness, we spin and twirl,
Chasing echoes, a cosmic whirl.
Gravity who? We bounce and play,
In the void, it's a field day!

The Allure of Light

Dancing beams, they whisper sweet,
In cosmic ballet, they twist and greet.
Light-years giggle, they join the fun,
   Chasing shadows, on the run!

Oh, the allure of shining rays,
Lighting up the silliest ways.
A supernova burst of cheer,
Let's hula hoop with stars right here!

Flashing colors, a vibrant sight,
Painting galaxies with delight.
Running toward a blazing sun,
   A race of laughter has begun!

With every flash, a joke we share,
As we zoom through the dazzling air.
Let's toast to starlight's glowing spark,
In this wild dance, we leave our mark!

Transcendent Travels

On a spaceship made of giggles and dreams,
We soar through galaxies, bursting at seams.
With a wink and a smile, we navigate time,
Silly tales echo, a cosmic rhyme!

Stardust sprinkled on our snack,
Cosmic candy in every pack.
Wait, is that a comet or a flying pie?
Let's take a bite and see it fly high!

We've got cosmic maps written in jokes,
The Milky Way laughs, as we poke.
With laughter echoing through astral halls,
We dance with planets, answering calls!

So grab your cap, let's make a scene,
In the universe, we reign supreme.
With every trip, a chuckle unfolds,
In this saga of laughs, adventure molds!

Beyond the Veil of Existence

I slipped through a door, no handle in sight,
Landed in slippers, how odd, what a flight!
A cat in a suit offered me tea,
Said, "Join the parade, you'll be late for the spree!"

Balloons filled with stardust danced in the air,
Each one claimed to have secrets to share.
I floated on giggles, a trampoline ride,
Then fell into laughter, my dignity fried.

The trees played the banjo, the grass made a stew,
While squirrels in bow ties debated the blue.
I juggled my worries, a sight to behold,
A cosmos of chaos wrapped up in pure gold.

With each step I took, the ground turned to cheese,
I chased after dreams that blew in on a breeze.
Reality wobbled, and I went along,
In a concert of quirks, they all sang my song.

Timeless Trails

I tripped on a clock that ticked to the beat,
Fantastic, yet strange, it danced on my feet.
With every tick-tock, the colors would change,
Past and future twirled, all wobbling strange.

I met a time traveler stuck in a loop,
He offered me pizza with extra weird soup.
"Just one more bite," he insisted with glee,
But I turned into jelly—now that's quite a spree!

We rode on a snail that claimed it was fast,
It burped with a fizzle, a time-bending blast.
We zoomed through the ages, from ribbons to pixels,
Each moment a riddle that wiggled and tickled.

Then splat! I arrived in a world made of cake,
Each friend was a muffin, how funny to bake!
With frosting for clouds and candy for rain,
I laughed and I played, I forgot all my pain.

Quantum Visions

I peered through the lens of a joke in my mind,
And saw all the particles having a bind.
Quarks played hopscotch on the back of a wave,
As laughter erupted, carefree and brave.

I built a machine out of gooey old foam,
It hummed silly tunes, calling particles home.
Each button I pressed sent me further through space,
Where fish wore afros and drove in a race!

I flipped through dimensions like flipping a dime,
On one side, I danced; on the other, I mime.
In this circus of quirks, gravity's a joke,
And time has a mustache—who said a frog spoke?

The universe chuckled, cosmic and wide,
As I rode on a comet, my giggles my guide.
In this odd little journey where laughter is king,
I found all my dreams made of silly string.

Beyond the Horizon of Reality

Past the edge of what's real, I teeter and sway,
On unicorn boats with no anchor to stay.
I sailed through a panorama of shrieks and delight,
While jellybean stars waddled off in the night.

The moon wore pajamas stitched with bright dreams,
Spilling marshmallow wishes in luminous beams.
I danced with the fireflies who taught me to glow,
In a world made of giggles and topped with a bow.

On the edge of the sea of forgotten old thoughts,
Where dolphins text messages in glittery spots.
I played with the sunset, flipped colors like cards,
And juggled the shadows like charming regards.

Reality grinned, it knew I was here,
In a place full of whimsy, no burdens, no fear.
Each moment a jest, with humor wrapped round,
In this zany adventure, joy knows no bound.

Horizon Hunters

We chase the edge where silly meets the stars,
With flip-flops on, we zoom past Mars.
Lunar burgers sizzling on a grill,
Who knew space snacks could give such a thrill?

With googly eyes and helmets made of cheese,
We prank the aliens with unearthly sneezes.
Our spaceship's name? The Laughter Cruiser,
Fully equipped with a rubber chicken user.

We surf the rays and dance on comets,
In our pajamas, flaunting cosmic garments.
The Milky Way's a stage for our routine,
A cosmic sitcom, you know what I mean?

When galactic giggles echo through the void,
We toast to mischief, oh how we enjoyed!
For every star, a wish, or maybe a pun,
Horizon hunting? Oh boy, so much fun!

The Uncharted Skies

Bouncing on clouds, we take to the air,
Sailing through giggles without a care.
Galactic maps with doodles and flair,
Adventure awaits; we can't help but stare.

Kites made of stardust, we fly high,
Playing catch with meteors as they zoom by.
Why do aliens giggle when we sing?
Maybe they're jealous of our rubber band fling!

Our rocket's a gadget from a thrift store,
Complete with stickers and an old sing-along score.
Navigating chaos with silly commands,
'Make a left at the giant candy lands!'

The cosmic playground is open, let's play,
With laughter and joy leading us astray.
Every nebula's a park filled with bliss,
In the uncharted skies, there's magic we can't miss!

Fractal Footsteps

Step into patterns of zany delight,
Where each tiny step spins colors so bright.
We hop on the waves of the fractal dance,
Painting the cosmos with every prance.

Twisting and doubling, our paths intertwine,
"Why's gravity slippery?" we laugh as we climb.
The ground is a riddle wrapped in a pun,
Dancing in loops 'til the day is all done.

Each footfall's a splash in the wibbly air,
Leapfrogging through dimensions with whimsical flair.
Shimmering doughnuts, what do they mean?
We giggle and tumble, chasin' the dream!

As fractals unfold in the backdrop of fun,
We're cartoonish phantoms, forever on the run.
Chasing our tails through infinity's game,
In this kaleidoscope world, we'll never be tame!

Radiant Rambles

On trails of twinkles, we stomp our way,
Through karaoke stars that sing and sway.
Aliens join us, with space-age tunes,
We boogie and stumble underneath the moons.

Picnicking on planets made of cake,
Bubblegum comets that twirl and shake.
'Pass the stardust, hold the pickles, please!'
Cosmic cuisine that'll knock you to your knees!

With laughing moons and silly sunbeams,
We chase our wildest, brightly-lit dreams.
Every corner a surprise, laughter ignites,
Rainbow lights guiding our whimsical flights.

From the edge of the cosmos, we relish the view,
Radiant rambles, oh, I love this crew!
So let's keep laughing, let's keep it absurd,
In the fabric of space, let our joy be heard!

www.ingramcontent.com/pod-product-compliance
Lightning Source LLC
Chambersburg PA
CBHW071839160426
43209CB00003B/347